INSIGHTS ON DEMAND®

Building Business
Success in the
On Demand Economy

By Frédéric-Charles Petit

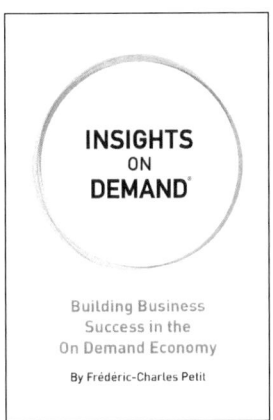

By Frédéric-Charles Petit

Published by ITWP
21 River Road
Wilton, CT 06897 US
t: +1 203 834 8585
f: +1 203 834 8686

www.itwpcompany.com/

© Frédéric-Charles Petit. All right reserved. Reproduction of any portion of this book is permitted for individual use if credit is given to Frédéric-Charles Petit. Systematic or multiple reproduction or distribution of any part of this book or inclusion of any material in publication for sale is permitted only with prior written permission of Frédéric-Charles Petit.

ISBN 978-0-578-44670-7
PRINTED IN THE UNITED KINGDOM

Editor: YourWriters.com

Design by Rob Hudgins & 5050 Design.com

TABLE OF CONTENTS

Introduction: Insights on Demand is a Promise, an Enabler and a Revolution 6

Chapter One: When Everything Changes 13

Chapter Two: The Continuing History of Market Research 23

Chapter Three: A Perfect Storm Changes the Global Marketplace Forever 29

Chapter Four: Advanced Technology is the Great Enabler and Equalizer 35

Chapter Five: Success in the On Demand Universe 47

Chapter Six: At the Heart of It All: The Individual Consumer 55

Chapter Seven: Futurecasting: Meeting Unimaginable Complexity with Insights on Demand 61

Appendix: About the Insights on Demand Consortium 71

INTRODUCTION

Insights on Demand: A Promise, an Enabler and a Revolution

Insights on Demand. Think about that term for just a moment.

First, it's a promise. A promise that we in the market research industry will deliver to our clients deep, meaningful consumer perceptions of their products and brands on-the-spot, when businesspeople need them most to support critical decision making, day in and day out. Not tomorrow or next week but right here, right now, in real time.

Secondly, the very concept itself is an enabler. We're talking about giving businesses the solid foundation they need to move ahead with key business activities like brand and product development and marketing campaign designs. And we're enabling them to do it at the breakneck speed of change in the global marketplace. Without that solid foundation under their feet, businesses lack the security they need to move forward into new, uncharted territory. Business stops dead in its tracks.

Thirdly, more than an evolution, it is a true revolution. Over time our industry has responded to the needs of business, always employing the latest technologies and techniques to give companies the decision-making support they need. As the marketplace has moved more and more toward an On Demand economy, it's not surprising that it has taken market research some time to move with it; history shows that there is always resistance to a paradigm shift of this magnitude. And, as the industry has moved to meet new demands, it has become clear that it's not enough JUST to deliver in real-time. WHAT is delivered has to be high quality; it has to be the right response to the need or it is of little value. (If someone ordered a pizza through the on-demand food-delivery company Just Eat, and a burrito was delivered instead, how valuable would the service really be?) In the end, Insights on Demand is not just an evolution because it impacts deeply the way companies need to organize their insights team. It is a reaction to the emergence of the On Demand economy.

That brings us to the definition of Insights on Demand: It is the tight integration of **advanced technology infused with world-class expertise, wide-ranging, global communities of consumers and the underlying market muscle of expert research professionals.** This distinctive hybrid is the perfect response to the needs of businesses in the new On Demand economy.

Advanced technology is the enabler—the engine that makes it possible to access product and brand insights in real time—when they REALLY matter in the On Demand economy. And it is also the great equalizer; technology makes consumer intent available to companies large and small, catapulting them instantly into the On Demand marketplace. This signifies the **democratization** of not just market research (MR), but also business as-a-whole. For businesses in MR it means adopting an organization where the center of gravity is not just the community of researchers, but includes engineers as well. Progress must involve people who can think, create, design and code world-class MR technology.

Wide-ranging, global communities of consumers are the repository of the **exact** insights businesses need to provide a solid foundation under their feet. Because communities encompass consumers in every geography and demographic, businesses can target the precise audiences they need to provide meaningful insights about their brands and products. Need to query mothers over thirty who are avid online shoppers to help in planning an online shopping special? They're there. (In other words, it's pizza WITH pepperoni and onions, not a burrito.)

The underlying expertise of market research professionals is part of the Insights on Demand equation. Our industry's professionals bring together advanced data collection and analytical tools, while enabling access to global consumer communities, creating the precise environment needed to result in Insights on Demand. You might say they have provided the gene that has made the continuing Insights on Demand (IoD) evolutionary process possible.

But there is a fundamental concept that needs to be emphasized: Insights on Demand is not SaaS, and neither is it the traditional, mediated way of conducting research. SaaS research software, such as survey software for instance, does not give the answer to any question, it is just a tool. Mediated market research is also not solving this critical need for instant information and knowledge of consumers. IoD is this new paradigm that does not replace SaaS or mediated research, but rather encompasses them by blending the best of both.

Insights on Demand is what will ensure that the promise is kept

As we said earlier, Insights on Demand, although in its infancy, is the promise to deliver meaningful consumer perceptions of their products and brands on-the-spot, when businesspeople need them most to support critical decision-making. That promise is rooted in our longstanding commitment to use the most advanced tools and methods at our disposal to give the business community the foundation it needs to drive into the future.

You can see that promise way back in the seminal period that is sometimes viewed as our industry's birth. It all started when Charles Parlin was hired by the Curtis Publishing Company in 1911. The company had purchased a magazine about agriculture, while knowing little about the subject. So they wanted Parlin to provide better insight into the market, the readers, and how best to advertise to the demographic. Parlin, previously a media commentator, interviewed "gentleman farmers" about when and where they bought agricultural products. Along the way he created his own techniques and figured out how to present findings to executives.

He then examined the retail store industry, producing a report called *Department Store Lines*, showing marketers how to maximize profits based on the goods they advertised. But the real coup came in 1914, when Parlin released a five-page study called *Automobiles*, with a clear focus on female buying habits. He used his data to correctly predict the future of auto sales, giving nascent auto manufacturers the insights they needed to pour dollars into advertising. And he eventually fathered the first-ever market research company, National Analysts.

As the industry grew through the last century, researchers nurtured the original commitment to use innovative research techniques and the latest technologies, providing businesses with the insights they needed to plan product/brand development and direct precious advertising dollars into the most promising areas. The industry has thrived because businesses know they can always count on their market research partners to use all the tools and expertise at their disposal to create a solid decision-making foundation under their feet.

A century later, the natural culmination of that promise is Insights on Demand.

Insights on Demand as the Enabler

Across the global marketplace and in every industry, businesses are in a minute-to-minute fight for survival. They constantly strive to operate faster, better and sometimes cheaper to retain footing on the constantly shifting sands. No strategy is good enough if its execution is not coping with the absolute necessity of adapting tactics almost every day.

Think about this: Home product manufacturers and retailers now compete with Amazon, which features same-day delivery in some metro areas. The company has even tried out a Prime Now service in Boston, featuring delivery in one-to-two hours. And there's something more: Amazon's augmented reality shopping. The AR View feature inside its iOS shopping app previews thousands of products in 3D, ranging from kitchen appliances to toys to electronics. Then there's Google Express, which now provides same-day delivery in some metro areas for a range of products, including electronics, clothing and home décor.

Bottom line? Forget about offering two-week delivery on goods. That's a one-way ticket to obsolescence. If a business is to keep up with precedent-shattering pace of change in the On Demand economy, it needs a secret weapon on its side.

Insights on Demand is the weapon that gives businesses the power (read: information) they need to continue to drive ahead in the On Demand marketplace. They know right here and right now (not two weeks from now) what their most important audiences need and how they need it delivered. This enables them to move forward with product/brand development plans knowing—not guessing—that their creations will be well-received in the marketplace.

In one instance, businesses are using the power of Insights on Demand to **literally** drive growth throughout merger and acquisition (M&A) processes. As the global bull market continues to drive M&A activity, companies need to know how to approach and structure potential partnerships and how the new entity will be received in the marketplace. Insights on Demand allows them to instantly access market intelligence to identify and vet partners, refine post-merger expansion strategy and build a strong global supply chain post-merger. Then, to ensure survival in the On Demand economy, newly merged companies turn to Insights on Demand for the immediate and ongoing understanding of the competitive landscape, channel distribution and consumer trends they need to make any necessary adjustments to strategic plans as the parties involved learn how best to work together to create a viable new company.

Of course, at the root of Insights on Demand's ability to enable business growth and ultimate survival is the advanced information/consumer enabling technology that makes it possible to instantly reach across the globe for the precise insights needed to support decision-making. In later chapters we'll look at some of the technologies powering Insights on Demand and how they are being used across the industry. As we said earlier, both large and small market research firms are using advanced tech to help support their clients' survival. We'll show you just how these companies are using tech to power the On Demand economy. And, through the power of Insights on Demand, these companies are also ensuring the survival of market research as a discipline.

Insights on Demand as the Culmination of an Evolutionary Process

When you think of any evolutionary process, it is clear development didn't happen overnight. It took humans millions of years to develop into who we are today; businesses and industries develop over decades;

and business processes are developed and refined as conditions around them—and thus business needs—change.

In fact, evolution always occurs in response to external pressures. (Think, for example, of the advancements in Ancient Egypt. They were the direct result of the Egyptians' need to control the annual flooding of the Nile. Without that pressure those advancements would never have been made.) Across global markets, there is a proliferation of new businesses shaking the established order, proving that size is no longer a guarantee of survival. So the pressures of the On Demand landscape—the need for companies to compete with the likes of large and small pioneers like Amazon, Marketo, Airbnb and Uber—have driven the need for businesses to have ongoing access to real-time, evolving consumer feedback driven by cost-effective technology that automates the delivery of those insights to speed up the decision-making process. In other words, Insights on Demand.

So Insights on Demand is the market research industry's logical—and necessary—response to changes in the marketplace, particularly the development of the global On Demand economy. (Through the course of this book we'll look in some detail at how these market forces have arisen and their impact on market research.) And it's important to note that, like all evolutionary processes, the growth and development of Insights on Demand will be ongoing as the market research industry continues to monitor and respond to always changing needs in the marketplace.

Bottom line: Insights on Demand is the way forward; it is what will transform and expand our industry and the business universe at-large. It is the democratization agent for market research. It is bigger than market research as we know it because it's broader and accessible to more organizations and more functions within an organization. Whether it is better is a question equivalent to asking whether a car is better than a carriage: It is a question of century, and clearly Insights on Demand is the wave of the future for business in the 21st century. Just as we have been for more than a century, the market research industry will be there as a guide into the future of business, but it cannot be there with the same old vanishing dogmas. The industry must change—at its very roots—to deliver on its promise to business.

CASE STUDY

Just Eat Uses the Power of Insights on Demand to Fuel Growth

Just Eat is one of the world's leading marketplaces for online food delivery. From humble beginnings in a Danish basement in 2001 to their 2014 listing on the London Stock Exchange, Just Eat now operates in 12 markets across the globe. The company has created a world of choice, serving everything from pizza to sushi and burgers to burritos. Connecting over 15 million customers with over 60,000 Restaurant Partners serving over 100 different cuisine types, they're working hard to deliver their vision to create the world's greatest food community.

The company is determined to take advantage of huge opportunities for growth, with its long-term ambition to *virtually* revolutionize the way people order and enjoy food. Toward that end and in one specific instance, marketers wanted to test two different TV advertising campaigns run on Spanish television. They needed the results to help them save time and advertising resources, helping them cement their leadership position in the fast-moving, ultra-competitive food delivery marketplace.

In a perfect example of how Insights on Demand can work to ensure a competitive edge, Just Eat marketers looked to PowerConcept, Toluna's fully automated, real-time concept testing tool to give them an on-the-spot view of consumer reactions to the two ad campaigns they tested.

The company used the advanced Toluna technology, part of the QuickSurveys platform, to test brand awareness and consumer behavior both before and after viewing the ads. The advanced technology and access to Toluna's global community (read: Insights on Demand) gave Just Eat marketers the real-time, reliable data they needed to support informed decision-making on what specific advertising deserved their time, attention and valuable resources. Armed with the strength of Insights on Demand, the Just Eat team was able to take the right advertising path toward ensuring its leadership role in one of its key markets.

CHAPTER 1

When Everything Changes...

A few years ago there was a popular book that hit the bestseller lists: *When Everything Changes, Change Everything.* The concept behind the book was that when crisis strikes in someone's personal or professional life, the most fruitful response is to meet the change with sweeping transformation, becoming a new person better suited to the new environment. Or, as naturalist Charles Darwin determined in his study of human and animal evolution, species most able to adapt are the survivors of the evolutionary chain. He once wrote, "In the long history of humankind (and animal kind, too) those who learned to collaborate and improvise most effectively have prevailed."

In today's global On Demand economy, everything has changed, and it is becoming more and more evident that only the most adaptive industries and businesses will survive. Of course the market research industry is hardly immune from what in some circles is being called the "uberification" of the marketplace. The term refers of course to the astronomical and transformational success of the transportation company Uber, which is changing not only how the transportation industry functions, but what consumers expect from any company, offering any kind of service.

The Uberfication of the Marketplace

Uber represents what is known in the technology industry as disruptive innovation. (In fact, the transportation industry is currently divided into the time before and the time after Uber.) On the surface, we think of a disruption as "an innovative business model that seeks to appeal to a new market or share of consumers, which, in doing so, unduly impacts an existing market and its consumers." But powerful disruptors like Uber actually do more than that. They transform the marketplace by creating a simpler, cheaper or more convenient product, service, or even a new translation of a product or service, literally creating a new demand in the market. (Think of the mobile web as an example. A few years ago it would have been inconceivable to have access to the Web wherever you go. Now it's inconceivable to every professional on the face of the planet not to have that kind of access.) Until recently, the rule was that a disruption was representative of a brand new product or service…but not anymore. Take Amazon as an example: It began life as simply an online book retailer, and by the time it was introduced in 1994 those were already a-dime-a-dozen in the online universe. But the form and scope it took—as a massive marketplace where retailers could reach an audience for literally any product on Earth— was unprecedented and changed the retail climate forever.

Again, Uber is just that kind of disruption. While it is a transportation company, or at least a transportation platform, it neither owns cars or other forms of transportation, nor hires drivers. In fact, (reminiscent of Amazon and its retailers) it simply allows independent drivers to earn money by using its platform to reach customers. In the strictest sense of the term, it is a ride-sharing company; drivers share space in their cars with riders who need to be ferried from Point A to Point B, somewhere in the driver's local area. You might say that, rather than being powered by fleets of taxis or limousines, the company is "app-driven." For Uber, its drivers and riders, it's all about the technology that allows a potential rider to summon and track a ride in the area, rather than waiting on a street corner (often for long periods) hailing cabs.

Another example of a response to the demand for more convenient transportation is BlaBlaCar, an online marketplace for carpools. Drivers and passengers use the service to arrange to travel together, sharing the cost of the trip. Like Uber, the company does not own any vehicles, and earns revenue through a commission system. Available across Europe, the company is actually named for a rating scale assessing drivers' chattiness.

(One thing to notice is that neither Uber, nor Amazon, nor Blablacar are software companies: they are the combination of cloud-based technology, domain expertise and communities.)

Uber's History

It was, in fact, the antiquated system of hailing a cab that served as the impetus for Uber's birth. It all started back in 2008 when co-founders Travis Kalanick and Garrett Camp were together at a conference in Paris and—as old friends will—were complaining about those things that get under your skin. Typical entrepreneurs, the duo was unwilling to sit idly by and wait for someone else to solve this global issue. Trial business models and initial funding soon followed and by 2010, the company already set a few black cars rolling in New York City, with San Francisco serving as the next host city. Uber now operates all over the globe, with cultural and market differences seemingly no barrier to the company's growth. At this writing the business is valued somewhere above $75 billion.

Another important point about Uber is that local and national regulations that could seemingly scuttle a company that strays so far from accepted norms have not sounded death knells for Uber (or, for that matter, its closest competitor, Lyft). That's partly because the company and its founders have proven adept at working with regulators to iron out issues like unfair pricing and taxation. But there's something more at play here: Uber and Lyft were almost destined to succeed because they solved problems: finding a way to get where you need to go easily and inexpensively, while at the same time offering income opportunities.

Of course, the ride-share companies have still faced their share of regulatory and practical potholes. Uber has fought some of the issues by claiming it is not in the transportation business, but rather should be classified as a communications company, thereby making it immune to transportation-related related regulation. Nevertheless, in several areas around the world Uber especially has been greeted by large groups of protesting taxi drivers and governmental bodies intent on applying restrictions. In some cases, the company has been able to negotiate its return, while in others regulations have stopped it dead in its tracks—for now. No one thinks that governmental bodies will be able to permanently forestall the demand for low-cost, convenient service companies like Uber and Lyft offer. Whenever there is a seismic shift in an industry (or in this case the marketplace at-large) it's likely because a problem shared by many people has been solved. In such a case, it's almost impossible to block the forces of change.

This is a perfect description for what is happening in the market research industry. There was a problem: It was no longer good enough for companies to wait at curbside for the consumer insights they needed to make critical business decisions. Without ready access to those insights, they were being left in the dust of the On Demand economy; the fast-moving On Demand marketplace was rendering obsolete an old system that took days or weeks to provide needed insights. Like Uber and transportation, Insights on Demand is proving a necessary solution to a problem. Part disruptive technology and an innovative combination of existing services, it is the beginning of a new era in market research. From this moment forward, clients will expect to do business in an entirely different way. Like Uber riders, citizens of the On Demand business world now expect to be served (in this case with deep consumer insights) exactly when and how they need them. And they know that, from this moment on, anyone without real-time insights will be left out in the cold.

Airbnb is one company that, a few years ago, learned the hard way that tapping into real-time consumer insights can avert disaster. See the sidebar at the end of this chapter for the Airbnb story.

On the other hand, some companies are using customer insights to stay informed about what their audiences expect (and demand) in the On Demand economy. One good example is Kraft.

Kraft, a brand that prides itself in being part of American family life for the past 100 years, recently embarked on a journey to speak with a unified purpose to support today's modern families. The company knew it needed to home-in on the true definition of a modern family and deliver a message of understanding of the challenges parents face, and how kids feel about home life. The brand seemed to have understood that parents are often tough on themselves, especially around the holidays, trying too hard to live up to their definition of a "perfect" family. So Kraft embarked on survey research to support this concept.

The company set out to determine how both parents and children felt about what it takes—given the pressures of modern life—to "family" effectively, with that definition to serve as the core of their new creative campaign. Using Toluna's QuickSurveys survey tool to ensure rapid turnaround (in keeping with Kraft's plan to launch the new campaign in the beginning of 2018), Toluna surveyed more than 1,000 parents and 1,000 children aged 8-17, with a series of questions designed to assess their feelings about togetherness and mealtimes.

The findings were used to create a concept that all families could get behind. Kraft believes parents don't have to be perfect to be great. Through the brand's #FamilyGreatly campaign, Kraft showed there is no one right way to family as long as people do it with love and conviction.

Not surprisingly, considering the pressures levied on modern parents, eight out of ten parents felt pressured to be perfect. But—here's the surprising part—four out of five of the kids surveyed said they'd rather have a "great" parent than a "perfect" one. (This result was the inspiration for the campaign's original title, "#FamilyGreatly.") Other results showed that—despite the pressure to be perfect—95 percent of the parents surveyed think everyone *should* be able to family in the best way they know how, as long as they do it with conviction. And although they agreed that no family is perfect, 86 percent of parents surveyed said "how we family is great." One data point critical to Kraft—confirming its continued role in family life—revealed that 80 percent of parents and 78 percent of kids believe mealtimes bring families together.

"Parents put a lot of pressure on themselves believing there is a perfect, or right way to family. The reality is there are a billion ways to #FamilyGreatly, and your way, if it's done with love and conviction, is the best way," said Anne Field, Director of Brand Building for Kraft. "When we first identified this insight, we knew it clearly spelled out what we believe as a brand. When we shared it with families, we felt such power in this universal truth. And as a mom of two young daughters and a daughter myself, I couldn't wait to share this message."

Using the survey findings as a guide, the company created an enormously touching video featuring real parents and children rather than professional actors, demonstrating parents' need to be perfect, balanced by their children's pure love.

By using data to inform creative concepts, brands like Kraft are putting consumers at the heart of their decision-making. This gives them the confidence to move forward, knowing their audience will be there with them when they do.

In a recent blog on the Huffington Post's web site, digital strategist Jure Klepic encapsulated the growing importance of Insights on Demand to today's businesses.

"As business has grown and evolved, marketers are all well aware that we can no longer try to give consumers 'any color they want, so long as it's black,' as Henry Ford was so fond of saying. Companies now realize that they need to offer a wide variety of products, services, colors and fashions to appeal to an ever-changing customer base. But why do some products fairly jump off the shelves while others languish in obscurity? Each company may assert that it has done in-depth market research, but have they truly looked for consumer insights which would make their product more desirable?

"Businesses need to culturally understand why each group is different. What was going on as each generation was growing up? What shaped their values and morals? How do they interact with each other and corporations? While an older generation might have been more open to accepting Ford's brusque evaluation, younger consumers will certainly not consent to any such arrangement. Added to the complex demographic puzzle is the new global economy where consumers can virtually come from any part of the world that has an Internet connection. All of this must also be accomplished in the blink of a virtual eye because the social media universe has made the consumer response swift and unrelenting."

In Chapter Two, we'll look at how the market research industry has continued to develop over more than 100 years. While some would say that in recent years the industry has been slow to respond to the needs of business in the On Demand economy, you'll see that the industry clearly has the right DNA to drive change.

CASE STUDY

Look Before You Leap into a Disastrous Campaign

As we've already pointed out, companies that are charter members of the On Demand economy are doing far more than just introducing new brands—they are actually forging new paths in their industries, and in some cases actually creating whole new industry segments. That's certainly the case with Airbnb, which has turned the hospitality industry on its head by pioneering a space-sharing app/ DIY home rental company. But if you're going to make forays into brand new areas, you'd better keep close tabs on your customers to know you're venturing into friendly territory.

Airbnb's marketing team learned that lesson when it embarked on a public relations campaign it thought consumers would find "cute and creative," without ever gauging customer insight to be sure their assessment was right.

The company produced a series of ads that literally bragged about the amount of taxes it pays to the city of San Francisco. One ad read: "Dear Public Library System, we hope you use some of the $12 million in hotel taxes to keep the library open later. Love, Airbnb." But there was no context to the ads, leaving some people confused. Others commented that they believed the company was bragging about the amount of money it made. No one seemed to view the ads with the light touch the marketing team intended, while at the same time portraying the company as a responsible citizen.

Airbnb spokesman Christopher Nulty actually apologized for the debacle in an article on VICE News. "The intent was to show the hotel tax contribution from our hosts and guests, which is roughly $1 million per month. It was the wrong tone, and we apologize to anyone who was offended. These ads are being taken down immediately."

Clearly, the fact that the company actually felt the need to submit an apology meant that the campaign had been a clear disaster. And the real disaster is that the whole incident could have been easily avoided. In retrospect, it seems obvious that the marketing team should have begun by asking the question, "Will our audience understand the thrust of the ads?" Team members should have understood that they were too close to the situation to judge customer sentiment—without actually going out to their consumers and polling sentiment.

This is where Insights on Demand comes in. With instant access to the targeted Airbnb audience, company marketers could have presented the campaign concept, gauged sentiment, and within hours discovered that their approach was almost universally disliked. They could then have easily shifted gears, saving time and money and preserving invaluable consumer good will. As it was, the company had to spend valuable resources retrenching and repairing critical customer relationships.

CHAPTER 2

The Continuing History of Market Research

As forces in the economy-at-large have driven change, market research has always been out front with innovative responses to those changes. This is the continuing promise of market research. While some would say the On Demand economy has driven past MR, the industry's history shows that it is in its DNA to continue to be the energizing force behind business. A look at market research through the years demonstrates that MR has always been a prime driver behind marketplace growth and evolution.

The Beginnings

Some business historians contend that market research has actually been around for centuries; businesspeople have always tried, in one way or another, to determine how customers felt about their goods and products. On the other hand, some experts claim that the modern-day understanding of market research was born in the early 1900s, with two important events. First, Herman Hollerith introduced punch cards to tabulate data collected through the U.S. Census, and *The Literary Digest* ran what is considered to be the very first national U.S. survey—to gauge support for presidential candidates.

Then there is the camp that declares Charles Coolidge Parlin the father of market research, because he collected information about various demographics, with the clear intent of understanding and documenting buying habits. Back in 1911, Parlin was hired by Curtis Publishing to help management understand what advertising would be most effective with purchasers of farm equipment. Over six months, he interviewed dozens of subjects and compiled a 460-page survey about how and where agricultural products were purchased. In the process, he figured out how to break down results and findings to easily understand pieces when presenting to executives.

Parlin then went on to produce a report about the department store industry, and eventually his piece de resistance, a study on the burgeoning auto industry that correctly predicted the future of the auto industry and became a virtual Bible for advertisers. He then went on to found what is often viewed as the very first market research company, National Analysts. He also coined the term *commercial research* to describe the fledgling industry. That term later morphed into the now familiar market research.

Here is a look at other key developments in the field.

- Two more early pioneers in the field were Daniel Starch and George Gallup. Starch developed the rule that advertising should only be considered effective when it met five criteria: it had to be seen, read, believed, recalled, and acted upon. And Gallup is of course famous for the poll that bears his name and is still a fixture in the market research industry. He also developed the system of *aided recall,* a system that followed along the lines of Starch's for determining the effectiveness of advertising. It involved interviewing people to see if they could remember an ad based on a series of triggers, while not being shown the ad itself. And during the same period, Rensis Likert developed the Likert Scale for measuring attitudinal differences.

- Then, in the 1940s, Robert Merton and Paul Lazarsfeld introduced focus groups as a method to obtain qualitative data. And also during that decade, marketing academic John Howard started including into his research perspectives from social sciences, such as psychology, sociology, anthropology, semiotics economics, and management science. Also during that period, the first ratings index was created for radio listeners and Ernest Dichter introduced a theory known as "motivational research," which was a precursor to what is known as brand equity (postulating that brands — and the products and services they are associated with — have an identity that influences perception, behavior, etc.).

- The 1950s and 1960s ushered in the age of television and other burgeoning technology. During the fifties, researchers began for the first time to automatically collect data through recording devices on TV sets. In the sixties, Compuserve created the first digital forum for customer feedback. Think of it as the ancestor of social media. And, in terms of technology development, here's a massive one: An arm of the U.S. Defense Department, the Advanced Research Projects Agency Network (or Arpanet) sent its first messages using TCP/IP protocol. This was to become the foundation of the Internet—the one technology that has completely transformed global commerce—of course reaching its long arm of influence into the market research industry. It was also during that decade that Marshall McLuhan coined the term "global village" to describe consumers' interactions with brands through telecommunications.

- Technological development continued through the 1970s and 1980s, with audio recordings added to focus groups for the first time in the early seventies. Then in the eighties the transformative development was the introduction of the first personal computer. That enabled researchers to engage in computer-assisted telephone interviewing (CATI) for the first time.

- With the 1990s came the first websites on the World Wide Web and the world will never be the same. In terms of the market research industry, widespread adoption of the web led to the establishment of online focus groups, computer-aided web interviewing and bulletin boards. Also during that period, market research analysis software was developed, making analysis more practical and cost-effective.

- The new millennium saw the integration of quantitative and qualitative research methods, thanks to a number of developments, including insight communities, social media, market research, Big Data Analytics, and smartphone-based market research.

Time for a Leap

The new millennium has been a time of dramatic change across the globe and in every industry. With the dawn of the new era, market research became an increasingly indispensable part of business, showing companies how to increase customer engagement, improve brand awareness and accelerate time-to-market. And advancements like mobile research, improved customer experiences and digital tracking have given businesspeople a close-up-and-personal view of consumer behavior.

Now market research is poised to use its penchant for change and innovation to respond to the need for dramatic change in the new On Demand economy. In the next chapter we'll look at some of the forces driving that change.

CASE STUDY

The Future of Research in the Age of Insights on Demand: It's All About Agility
Susan Vidler, Head of Research, Harris Interactive UK

As the marketplace and MR industry changes in the wake of the On Demand economy, the role of research is being transformed.

Companies have begun to do business and make decisions at a much faster pace and have therefore been looking to researchers to provide insights more quickly. Over just the last six months or year, the pace of that change has accelerated dramatically.

One factor driving change is of course the spread of knowledge technologies; brands and organizations have come to expect answers to questions almost immediately. Within the research and insights industry those same technologies are enabling faster responses than ever before.

Researchers need to be ready to provide answers when their clients need them. They should be ready to respond whether clients need help with day-to-day tactical issues, or more strategic, complex business decisions. More and more, researchers are asked to provide answers to questions or business issues, often overnight or even in just a few hours where feasible. They need to develop the agility to respond quickly—whatever is being asked of them. That obviously means putting a number of different processes in place— including, of course, the most advanced technologies.

It certainly seems clear that the role of automation in research will only increase and deepen. While, in some cases, that may mean a diminished role for some traditional research processes, I believe the new era actually presents opportunities to expand the role of research. For one thing, brands and organizations need researchers' expertise to help them interpret and understand the vast amounts of information produced through knowledge technologies.

In addition, market research professionals have a role to play in designing the products that brands use to automate their research processes, to ensure that the rigor and quality required is embedded within the design of the tools used. Again, there is real value in the specialized expertise insight professionals can bring to product design; they understand how to structure research programs and how the insights garnered should be understood. But researchers need to embrace, and most of them do, the emergence of AI-powered research and replication through algorithm.

CHAPTER 3

A Perfect Storm Changes the Global Marketplace Forever

Over the past few years, the global marketplace has seen a number of dramatic changes that—taken together—have created a perfect storm impacting the way companies do business. And, as the pace of change continues to accelerate, it has become increasingly clear that businesses need a tool in their back pockets that will give them insight into their most important customers' constantly changing needs.

Globalization of Business

Businesses are now competing with counterparts down the street and half a world away, making it critical that they gain consumer insights faster than ever before, in order to have the security they need to move forward with product or campaign development. But that urgency has been coupled with ever-tightening budgets and streamlined internal processes as companies seek to stay ahead of a growing field of competitors.

Changes in technology are of course a huge factor in promoting change in the global marketplace, driving both businesses and consumers to expect almost instantaneous delivery on the promise of instant gratification. Some businesses now are forced to deal with—and understand—competition in places where it never existed before, including in emerging markets around the world.

As a recent article in *Financial Times* noted, "First, businesses are having to respond faster than before. For example, a group with a Europe-wide pay freeze may have to be flexible enough to authorize salary increases to specialists and managers in developing countries, who are still able to jump ship for a better offer. Darryl Green, Asia President for Manpower Group, the recruitment agency, says: 'Countries where people move easily – such as India – are seeing executive pay rising rapidly. The sight of [well-paid] expatriate foreign managers inspires local people to ask for more. Employers have to respond.' Second, chief executives are focusing on a broader range of challenges and opportunities than ever before. With emerging-market companies as well as established multinationals as rivals, there is no time to waste. A case in point today is Africa, where rapid growth in key countries, notably Nigeria, has persuaded many business people that the continent's time may finally have arrived."

Particularly note the sentence, "With emerging-market companies as well as established multinationals as rivals, there is no time to waste." Executives, product marketers and insight professionals in companies of every size are finding that there is no time to waste, as unexpected competitors are suddenly snapping at their heels. One good definition of global competition comes from Arthur Thompson, A.J. Strickland, and John Gamble, successful business executives who have co-written more than a dozen educational books on business strategies. "Global competition exists when competitive conditions across national markets are linked strongly enough to form a true world market and when leading competitors compete head-to-head in many different countries."

Cost Pressures Driving Change

One major impact of global competition has been constantly increasing pressure to reduce costs, especially in businesses where price is a major differentiator in perceived value. One good example is the worldwide tire industry, which has been under intense cost pressure in recent years, as companies have struggled to convince consumers it really does matter which pieces of rubber anchor their cars to the road.

Technology is one great driver of cost reduction. Going back to the Industrial Revolution, we see how new technology and automation enabled mass production, leading to cost reduction per unit price. Think of Henry Ford and his assembly line, enabling him to produce cars Americans could finally afford. (More on this in Chapter Four.)

Another factor creating cost reduction pressure is competition from businesses in emerging markets. More often than not, labor and other production costs are less in developing countries, enabling local manufacturers to produce goods more inexpensively than their counterparts in the developed world.

That means businesses can no longer dedicate unlimited time and resources to market research studies; they need insights right now and for the right price in order for those insights to have any competitive value. Expensive and lengthy studies that guarantee 100 percent certainty are a thing of the past. Corporate marketers need to move forward quickly and with a high degree of confidence in their results. *"Pristine research" is not selling anymore. I know that when I write this, I will create controversy. But the reality is that good enough immediately is better than pristine. But good enough does not mean lower quality.*

Bringing Research and Planning In-House

One way companies are dealing with the intense cost and competitive pressure is by bringing more and more research and media planning functions in-house. A perfect example is Procter and Gamble, the world's biggest ad purchaser. In recent years the company has brought an ever-increasing number of functions in-house, with Chief Financial Officer Joe Moeller announcing recently, "We'll automate more media planning, production and distribution, bringing more of it in-house," he said. That is a continuation of an effort that has already cut the company's agency and production costs by $750 million annually in recent years.

Note that P&G's CFO specifically credited automation in the company's ability to bring functions in-house. More and more—thanks to advanced technology--companies are able to put research projects in the hands of in-house insight professionals, saving valuable time and resources.

In the following segment, Mark Uttley, Group Strategy Director at innovation company AKQA, identifies three major factors driving change in the market research industry.

Disruption, Data Science and CX Agents of Change

According to Uttley, the following factors are at the root of change in the market research industry.

- The disruptive influence of accelerated innovation

- The incursion of data science

- The influence of CX (Customer Experience)

Disruption

Every industry eventually faces the disruptive force of innovation, so it's no surprise—especially in an age of intense technical advancement—that market research is dealing with the disruptive force of change. However, the industry has been somewhat blindsided by the rate of change and origin of some disruptive forces.

"Disruption from accelerated innovation is coming from some unexpected categories—places it hasn't been before," Uttley says. "For example, Google and LinkedIn are offering research services they haven't offered before. This kind of disruption can do a lot of damage to an industry."

He goes on to note that certain social media sites have begun to offer a variety of research methodologies, including psychographic segmentation, which involves dividing a market into segments based upon different personality traits, values, attitudes, interests, and lifestyles of consumers. "In many cases the results of this kind of segmentation are not very accurate," he observes. On the other hand, cluster analysis, which is the product of at least two different quantitative fields: statistics and machine learning, "represents a major step forward toward a next-level understanding of factors that drive consumer behavior," he says.

New entrants into the field are creating disruption he says, by continuing to develop and deploy machine learning techniques. "The most critical advancements are tools that link survey and behavioral data, providing a complete picture of consumer behavior. Advancement in this area is only going to continue, leading to more disruption in the industry."

Data Science

Uttley notes that the daily avalanche of data in the online universe has dramatically increased the importance of data science as a guide toward understanding what all this information really means. He points to the book, *Everybody Lies: Big Data, New Data, and What the Internet Can Tell Us About Who We Really Are,* as a great descriptor of the often unfathomable deluge of data. As the book's Amazon description notes, "By the end of an average day in the early twenty-first century, human beings searching the Internet will amass eight trillion gigabytes of data. This staggering amount of information—unprecedented in history—can tell us a great deal about who we are—the fears, desires, and behaviors that drive us, and the conscious and unconscious decisions we make. From the profound to the mundane, we can gain astonishing knowledge about the human psyche that less than twenty years ago, seemed unfathomable."

Despite the sheer magnitude of data available, researchers—like everyone else—are often unsure exactly what data has real value and what to reject. That's where data scientists can provide invaluable counsel, Uttley says. "This is a time in history when market researchers and data scientists need to be working together on multi-disciplinary teams. While researchers can come up with a hypotheses of how consumers might behave, they need an understanding of available data to get the most complete picture."

He asserts that while, "data science is not a panacea," it can help researchers zero in on the data that will be most helpful in developing a true and complete picture of consumer behavior. (We'll look at technologies impacting the market research industry in much more detail in the next chapter.)

CX

The third agent of change Uttley highlights is CX market research. Rather than focusing on a single transaction—a survey for example—CX aims to chart the course of a customer's journey to create a map clearly delineating behavior.

"CX is increasingly coming into play as clients demand insights in real time; time-consuming major surveys are becoming a thing of the past," he says. He notes that this is especially true for product organizations that need to make instantaneous decisions about product design and language.

As a result of this constantly increasing pressure, CX professionals on client-side research teams are often using CX methodologies that virtually eliminate the role of traditional market research. The industry must respond to this challenge, he says, by providing more efficient and timely access to insights from research panels. "In this day and age, I (as a client) should be able to access a panel of just the audience members I need, quickly and easily. The technology is there; it shouldn't be a difficult thing. In the future, that will have to change across the market research industry."

As Uttley observes, a look at these three major agents of change provides a snapshot of the shifting sands in the market research industry, leading inevitably to the need for Insights on Demand.

In the next chapter we'll focus more attention on one factor that has been a huge driver of change: technology. We'll explore the impact of technological change in individual industries and its monumental impact on the global marketplace—where it acts as a powerful engine driving the forces of change in the market research industry.

CHAPTER 4

Advanced Technology is the Great Enabler and Equalizer

Advanced technologies are making it possible for even small companies to develop deep profiles of their most important customers. Technologies like digital tracking provide clear roadmaps of consumers' online behavior, while digital assistants and AI jump to the future tense—allowing companies a view of customer intent. The range of technologies driving market research into the future continues to multiply exponentially. (I'll deal with one of the newer entries on that list, blockchain technology, later in the book as part of some future-casting.)

More than ever before, technology is allowing researchers and marketers to get to the vital information they need in record-time, making it possible for them to respond to the shifting sands in the marketplace.

A Mobile Society

Mobile technology has been one of the biggest factors impacting the market research industry. Thanks to the ubiquitous nature of the tech, we are now able to follow respondents as they travel from the real world into the digital and back again through digital tracking, gaining a true picture of their lives.

And on the qualitative side of the coin, the convenience of mobile surveys means that we now have a greatly expanded pool of respondents ready, willing and able to participate in surveys. It's no longer necessary to meet participants at some central locale (or even in their homes via landlines). And, as more and more consumers in the developing world jump on the mobile bandwagon, we'll be able to join them on their digital journeys. These platforms allow respondents to conduct a range of related activities, including video/mobile diaries, interactive social news feeds, creative collages, journey mapping and webcam in-depth interviews.

Automation: Making Data Available Even to Small Companies

It used to be that automation just facilitated data collection and field execution. But now automated systems are being applied to the whole range of market research functions across platforms that clients can access from anywhere. A good example is the TolunaInsights platform, an end-to-end market research solution. There are myriad benefits to this kind of automation, with time and cost savings at the top of this list. Insight professionals who are now dealing with constantly shrinking timelines and budgets are able to mount surveys at a moment's notice, in order to test products and concepts throughout a development project, using a "fast-fail" methodology. Using this approach, time- and cost-constrained researchers choose immediacy and cost-effectiveness over 100 percent certainty of results. Businesspeople everywhere now understand that perfection is of little use if deadlines for getting a product to market are missed.

Automation is proving to be a huge factor in the democratization of market research, as companies of every shape and size are now finding they can cost-effectively gain the insights they need to compete effectively.

Machine Leaning and Market Segmentation

Machine learning/artificial intelligence is another technology that promises to transform the face of customer insight research. Machine learning uses algorithms that actually learn from data, for instance, by continuously improving the prediction of future consumer behavior, with increasing levels of accuracy as the volumes of data increase.

The prominent technology consultancy IDC predicts that spending on AI software for marketing and related function businesses will grow at an exceptionally fast cumulative average growth rate (CAGR) of 54 percent worldwide, from around $360 million in 2016 to over $2 billion in 2020, due to the attractiveness of this technology to both sell-side suppliers and buy-side end-user customers. AI programs can literally measure what customers are doing at any point in time and predict what their next movements will be. It automates the market segmentation process, identifying priority customer groups for targeting, highlighting the opportunities they represent, and creating new clusters of interesting potential customers for attention.

Machine learning uncovers customer behavior patterns using real-time analysis, for example, of web site visitors' browsing behavior, page views, and product purchases. Profiles are continuously updated to provide a true reflection of real-time customer experiences and potential customer needs. Machine learning excels at handling uncertain and contradictory customer data and places results in a visual, easily consumable format.

In terms of segmentation, AI actually organizes customer profiles into buckets of customers with like behavior. It identifies segments with untapped potential, and it can even offer fixes for behavior that interrupts a path to purchase. For example, it may prescribe more social media "touchpoints" (advertising) along the path to purchase of a particular segment.

And there seems to be an unending flow of new ways to integrate machine learning and artificial intelligence into research methodologies. One emerging application is an online approach that creates a live chat conversation in place of or as a supplement to a survey as a way to develop deeper open-ended feedback. The program interprets the written comments and responds with a related probe to get deeper feedback. This approach uses text analytics to automatically code responses and allows you to get hybrid qual-quant insights in one study.

In the final analysis, AI is an almost unbelievably valuable tool for creating, understanding and acting on total addressable markets (TAMs). And it has arrived at just the right time—when researchers and marketers had hit a wall in terms of increasing their ability to predict consumer behavior. So it's certainly a tool that will—and should—be embraced to help consumer insight professionals show their customers how to reach their untapped markets.

Digital Tracking: Recording a Consumer's Path to Purchase

Changes in technology are of course a huge factor in promoting change in the global marketplace, driving both businesses and consumers to expect almost instantaneous delivery on the promise of "better, faster, cheaper." And if one source for goods and services can't deliver on the promise, consumers are more than willing to look elsewhere. Think about it: If a consumer can't find exactly the shade of lipstick she wants on a site like Walgreen's, there are plenty of other places she can go—some that, on the face of it, seem unlikely. Today, advanced digital tracking technology gives marketers the objective data they need to map a consumer's often circuitous path to purchase.

Digital tracking provides a precise record of what a consumer is doing online at any given moment, rather than a close approximation. Advanced tracking technology allows a marketing team to track a target population's online search activity, e-commerce website activity, and shopping cart activity, in the process creating a comprehensive online journey enabling them to better understand **how, when and why** consumers purchased their product. This can be an invaluable ally in determining how to use digital marketing spend.

In one example of how companies are using the technology to get the most impact from their spend, a leading CPG company wanted to increase online revenue among the specific target of 25-35 year old primary grocery shoppers. By gaining a clearer understanding of their target segment's online behavior, they wanted to develop a cohesive digital marketing strategy to reach these customers when and where they spend their time online, and with content and promotions best suited to trigger a purchase. Following the study, marketers were able to create a roadmap of the route consumers took that led to a purchase. Their digital strategies and spend were tailored as a result, which led to an increase in their e-commerce sales.

Here's an interesting note: Subjects in behavioral studies have often reported they found digital tracking much less intrusive in their lives than keeping track of their own actions.

Part of the Continuum

It's important to note that digital tracking and the resulting behavioral data are part of a continuum in next-generation insight gathering. In the case of the CPG study, for example, a group of likely consumers would be targeted and invited to join the study. Using a vehicle like Toluna's QuickSurveys, brand marketers could then query respondents, further segmenting the group based on the developing profile of their ideal subject. This new group could then be invited to join the digital tracking study. The behavioral data garnered from this very targeted group is infused into other study data to enrich results and give marketers a clear path forward.

In one perfect example of how marketers are using digital tracking as part of a blended approach, a large, global packaging company wanted to understand how consumers shop online for groceries in specific categories: milk, vegetables, laundry. They also wanted to understand if there is a difference in products being purchased online vs. offline shopping. Toward that end, they employed a combined quantitative, behavioral and qualitative approach. (Toluna QuickSurveys was used for screening and claimed behavior, Digital Tracking for collecting behavioral data, and QuickCommunities was utilized for qualitative behavior based on real actions.) In the end, the hybrid approach gave them invaluable information about their target audience's shopping patterns, informing decision-making about package design and the value of online and offline partnerships.

Typically, researchers now use a number of products (or an all-in-one insights platform like TolunaInsights) to gain a complete picture of consumer behavior. And, while digital tracking is generally just one component of a complete solution, more and more often it is becoming an indispensable part of the whole.

In a study designed to shed a bright light on shoppers' online paths to purchase, Toluna used its digital tracking solution to track the online behavior of 1,300 U.S. consumers for the forty-five days that constituted the 2017 holiday shopping season. The result was a treasure trove of more than four million hours of shopping, video binging, social media sharing and other surfing data. More importantly, those 1,300 panelists are representative of more than 174 million consumers like them, making the data a snapshot of a critical swath of American consumers.

"Because so many people are shopping online at that time of year, it makes the data incredibly powerful," comments Jay Rampuria, Executive Vice President, ITWP Group. "This project really allowed us to see how people truly engage with brands, their path to purchase, media consumption, the impact of various elements of marketing attribution, and more. This amount and depth of information would have been impossible even three of four years ago."

The data clarifies a number of issues important to retailers, with sometimes surprising information about paths to purchase near the top of the list. For example, stats show that (**not surprisingly**) Amazon outpaces all other shopping websites in regard to traffic, with consumers spending nearly 2.5 times more total hours shopping on Amazon than any other shopping site. But, in the eyebrow-raising column, YouTube videos/shows grabbed more of the panelists' attention than other video streaming services, by far, with consumers spending more than 15,500 hours watching YouTube during the shopping period.

The study even offered a window on individual online shopping behavior.

"It's harder and harder for retailers to understand what motivates consumers. They need to look at both the 'what' and the 'why' behind how people finally reach a purchase. This kind of data can help them understand what drives previously unpredictable consumers," he says.

He points to another stat that he says "will keep marketing and product managers up at night." Data from the study shows that consumers "load up" their shopping carts only to abandon more than 85 percent of the items in the cart at check out.

"The question marketing and product managers must now answer – or even face – is why people 'dump' products at the end when they felt enough affinity to pick up the item in the moment," Rampuria notes. "Imagine walking through a store, loading up the cart, and then returning everything back to their shelves."

Additionally, on Black Friday, one pharmacy/retailer customer—who eventually purchased $40 worth of lipstick on the retailer's site—had actually logged into twenty other retail sites on her path to purchase.

"If you're going to be successful in the online universe, you need to be ready to use the technology at your disposal to redefine not only the needle, but actually the haystack. Digital Tracking, especially when coupled with the ability to delve deeper into the 'why' with survey research, is one tool we're using to find that haystack," Rampuria concludes.

Of course, the transformative impact of technology on markets is not really new. One perfect example is the auto industry which, at a given point in time, was positioned for a leap into the future. Here's a look at that important moment in technology history.

Time Travel: The Transformative Effects of Technology on Other Industries

There is a quote by Oren Harari, business professor and author, that I think captures that moment when an industry or society sprints forward into a new stage. "The electric lightbulb didn't come from the continuous improvement of candles." In other words, it takes a leap in innovation to drive an industry forward. Think of the difference between a horse-drawn carriage and a car; the move to mechanize cars represented a dramatic shift in thinking that had little to do with the kind of "horsepower" that preceded it.

In fact, the auto industry is the perfect example of the transformative effects of technology.

Of course the idea to mechanize vehicles didn't grow out of thin air. Back in the 16th century Leonardo Da Vinci was sketching images of mechanized, horseless carriages. Like so many of the ideas that sprang from his fertile imagination, his vehicles were never actually built. It took a Frenchman, Nicholas-Joseph Cugnot, to build a self-propelled vehicle in 1769.

But when you chart the history of the automobile, you eventually get to Karl Benz and his Motor Car No. 1, what many historians have called the missing link between cars and horse-drawn buggies. **This represented a leap away from incremental improvement into an entirely new realm.** This three-wheeled car, known as the "Motorwagen" was patented in 1886. Benz also patented his own throttle system, spark plugs, gear shifters, a water radiator, a carburetor and other fundamentals to the automobile. And, of course, Benz eventually built a car company that still exists today as the Daimler Group.

So the Benz Motorwagen represented the first leap forward in creating the foundations of the modern auto industry. The second came almost thirty years later when, in 1913, Henry Ford first automated the manufacturing process of automobile construction. While he didn't invent the concept of the assembly line, he was the first to get it up and running in a manufacturing setting, literally giving birth to the modern automobile industry. Before Ford installed his line, it took workers more than twelve hours to assemble a car, with the line it took them two and one-half.

Once Ford employed his assembly line, he was able to produce more vehicles, allowing him to reduce the price of an auto. That made it possible to make vehicles available to the country's growing middle class, dramatically driving up the number of cars being produced, further reducing the relative cost of a car. **It's clear to see how technological advancement has a viral effect on progress in any industry, driving development forward on a number of fronts,**

Fast forward to the modern era of manufacturing, and we see that automation is quickly becoming the next big leap forward in vehicle construction. Welding robots make short and precise work of large, time-consuming processes, and the advent of machinery to lift and transport engine components, body panels and other integral parts of the cars themselves make things even more efficient. Without technology, cars would still be primitive, motorized boxes on top of steel frames.

And of course technology has had a huge impact on manufacturers' ability to produce safer vehicles. Advancements like reverse engineering and AI mean manufacturers can test possible safety features before incorporating them into their vehicles. Take for example the development of the automated driverless vehicle. The technology has the potential to revolutionize the auto industry—yet again—by making human beings perpetual and safer passengers in all vehicles.

Clearly, the auto industry is a prime example of a sector that has been transformed by technology-driven leaps in development. In an example of another industry, the media industry has been an early and enthusiastic adopter of technology, leading directly to its embrace of Insights on Demand.

Media Companies Paint Clear Picture of Insights on Demand

A Google listing for an Australia-based media/advertising agency, Sparcmedia, encapsulates the landscape in the media industry today. Under the header "Digital Advertising Agency," the listing reads, "Advertising Intelligence. Insights on your brand, competition, audience and media performance using research and in-depth strategic analysis. Get a clear and deep understanding of how these interlinking elements contribute to advertising success."

Media agencies like Sparc are proving just how far ahead of the tech curve they are, in using advanced technologies like automation and artificial intelligence to help inform media buys and placement. And, working with market research companies like Toluna, they are integrating deep consumer insights into their strategic analyses, quickly and cost-effectively guiding their clients to the best ways to capture the attention of their target audiences. This privileged access to advertising and market intelligence—unavailable until just a few years ago—gives agencies' clients an invaluable competitive edge.

And, with the advent of digital/social media, media companies—and especially content providers—watched ad revenues decline, threatening the existence of a whole industry. As a means of streamlining operations, cutting costs and facilitating research, companies like CNN, the BBC and *The New York Times* have automated a number of functions in the newsroom, while logically expanding tech advancement to the business/advertising side of operations. Some examples of automation in media companies include:

- The BBC's Juicer, an AI application that streamlines media workflows and lets journalists focus on reporting.

- Reuter's News Tracer, which can track down breaking news, so that journalists can limit mundane tasks.

- *The New York Times* Research and Development Lab's Editor app, which allows reporters to crunch more data faster.

And, in providers' ad departments, researchers are using these advanced capabilities to zero-in on the most effective, targeted advertising options for their advertisers. Like their counterparts in the agency world, they are providing, "Advertising Intelligence, insights on their brand, competition, audience and media performance using research and in-depth strategic analysis, providing a clear and deep understanding of how these interlinking elements contribute to advertising success."

The success of media companies' approach should stand as a lesson to other industries. For example, in 2016 total revenue across Fox News, CNN and MSNBC increased by almost 20 percent to a total of nearly $5 billion. This includes the two main sources of revenue: advertising and subscriber/licensing fees. This in an industry that was all-but given up for dead a few years ago. This is just one more example of the power of Insights on Demand in today's fast-moving global economy.

I believe it's time for the market research industry to follow the lead of media, automotive and other industries who have made dramatic leaps forward in development, so often using technology to get there.

In the next chapter we'll look at a range of companies and industries that—like the auto industry in an earlier era—have responded effectively to the need for change. These companies and industries offer a clear view of the On Demand economy as it continues to evolve.

CHAPTER 5

Success in the On Demand Universe

In this chapter we'll look at a number of companies and industries that have effectively changed to meet the demands of the new economy. Here are profiles of several On Demand companies that, taken together draw a clear picture of the On Demand Universe. They responded to needs in their marketspaces and found unique ways to give consumers the convenience and price advantage they were demanding.

Careem

Careem is being called the Uber of the Middle East. It is based in Dubai, and as of 2017 was operating in eighty cities in the Middle East, North Africa and South Asia. It actually began life as a corporate car booking service, then evolved into an Uber clone, with rides available for non-corporate clients. In keeping with the democratizing effects of On Demand companies, the service hires women drivers across its service area, estimating a female workforce of 20,000 by 2020, and prides itself on its generosity to freelance drivers. In fact, in a recent interview, the company's co-founder, Magnus Olsson, called Careem's drivers "captains" and discussed some of the benefits—including medical insurance and internships in some markets—being offered to the people at the helms of Careem's "ships."

"We ... believe we have a great product ... at the end of the day you're sitting in a car with a captain that drives you, and 80, 90 percent of the experience depends on the captain ... if we want riders to have a great experience we need to care for captains and make them partners in our success."

Drizly

So you've had a tough week, finally make it home, put your feet up and settle in for an evening of binge watching on Netflix. A glass or two of wine would go down really well, but the wine cupboard is bare and you have no intention of rousing yourself to schlep down to the local package store. So you pull up the Drizly app on your phone and order a nice Shiraz to smooth your ragged edges. It will be delivered to your door in less than one hour. Problem solved!

Like all On Demand companies, the Boston-based Drizly is a problem solver. And it is now solving problems for liquor merchants, as well as consumers. The Drizly app now shows consumers different prices on the beer, wine and liquor that they're looking for at local shops, along with different delivery or pick-up options, helping merchants connect with their customers. And stores can pay a monthly fee to use the Drizly app to sell directly to their thirsty customers. Back on the consumer side of the street, Drizly provides personalized recommendations for its users.

A recent TechCrunch article noted that, like most On Demand companies, Drizly is rooted in advanced technology. "Drizly operates in a very similar manner to Uber, providing the technology infrastructure that allows liquor retailers the opportunity to provide their own on-demand service, as well as an e-commerce platform through Drizly Connect."

On Demand Home Services Cleaning Up

The figure is staggering: The U.S. On Demand home services sector is now estimated at $600 billion. $600 billion! Leading companies in the sector include:

- Handy

- Hello Alfred

- Helpling

- YourMechanic

- Zaarly

These and dozens of other homecare services in the sector appeal directly to technology-savvy millennials who are inclined to run their homes like businesses and demand the convenience of accessing the services they need through web-based or mobile apps. And, with millennials slated to make up 75 percent of the U.S. workforce by 2025 (according to recent figures from *Forbes*), demand for technology-heavy services like these will only increase.

Take Handy as an example. The two-sided web-based/mobile app connects consumers with a range of local providers of homecare services. The company is in cities across the U.S., in Canada and the United Kingdom. Thousands of homecare providers use its platform to connect to the consumers who need their services. In another demonstration of the influence of technology on the sector, users can book Handy services by using Amazon Echo's voice-activated features. And in 2017 the company partnered with online retailer Wayfair to offer furniture installation and assembly as a feature when purchasing Wayfair furniture.

Then there's Streem, a true technology pioneer. The company uses a combination of augmented reality (which superimposes computerized enhancements on real-life images) and intelligent video, to beam a service provider directly to a job site no matter where the site is. The contractor is then able to provide an accurate price quote, based on how a job will eventually flesh out in the real world. So busy homeowners no longer have to wait for contractors, and contractors can greatly increase the number of quotes they can complete in a day.

In describing Streem's services, CEO Ryan Fink said in a statement. "For the consumer, that means not having to wait days, or sometimes weeks, for a professional to go on-site for an in-person quote or support. We're bringing home services into the On Demand economy."

PostMates

Want it all in one place? You can find it at PostMates, the logistics company that delivers just about anything, from restaurant take-out, to alcohol, to that birthday gift you forgot to pick up.

Despite being part of the On Demand economy, the company prides itself in being rooted in local communities. In fact, Postmates co-founder Bastian Lehmann calls the company the anti-Amazon. He recently said, "Amazon comes along and builds a warehouse outside a city. We like to say the city's our warehouse. We try to understand the inventory available, hacking the city, and having a fleet of delivery people that distribute these inventories." One way the company has been serving its local markets is with an app that allows small businesses to compete for business with larger enterprises like Amazon.

The company now operates in markets across the U.S., and recently began deliveries in Mexico City, its first location outside the U.S.

UrbanSitter

While many of the millennials who are powering the On Demand economy are either choosing to have children later or rejecting parenting altogether, those who are procreating want the childcare services they need at their fingertips. The San Francisco-based On Demand company, UrbanSitter, allows parents to search, vet and book childcare, including babysitters and nannies. And, on the other side of the app, providers can set up an account listing all their qualifications, so parents can find them. And, in keeping with its techie roots, the service interfaces with a number of social media platforms, including Facebook, so parents can determine if any of their contacts have contracted with a particular provider in their area.

In describing her impetus for starting the company, CEO and co-founder Lynn Perkins said, "I just thought it was kind of ridiculous that you could go to OpenTable and book a restaurant, but when you actually go to find a sitter, it would take you hours and days."

TaskRabbit

TaskRabbit "taskers" will take on any of those annoying little jobs you'd rather contract out than do yourself. That could include anything from assembling furniture, to grocery shopping, to yard work, to plumbing and electrical work. And for their trouble, taskers are rewarded with a flexible work schedule and—in some cases—a very livable income. In fact, some contractors report earning up to $2,000 a week.

The company actually began life in Boston in 2008, as RunMyErrand, changing its name in 2011. Over the next couple of years, the company experienced a decrease in bookings in the U.S. So management debuted a new model in London as a tryout. Rather than being based on an Ebay-style bidding format, the company allowed taskers to set their own rates, with the first to respond to a request taking on the work. The new system rescued the company from its doldrums, and in September 2017 IKEA Group acquired the company.

In an interview in *Forbes*, company CEO Stacy Brown-Philpot talked about the immersion of her company in technology—a characteristic of On Demand companies.

"We are unique because we've really invested in building a two-sided marketplace…We have about 30,000 people who show up at our site every month who want to task on TaskRabbit…The next step is machine learning and AI (artificial intelligence). And in the future, your filter in your refrigerator will run out and need to be changed, and you'll automatically get a Tasker to come and change it for you."

Udemy

Udemy's name is meant to stand for The Academy of You. The ultra-successful learning supermarket can trace its humble beginnings to 2007 when founder Eren Bali built software for a live virtual classroom while living in Turkey. Now a part of the massive open online course (MOOC) movement, the company currently offers 65,000 courses, with some offered free and some fee-based, depending on requirements of individual instructors.

Udemy courses include business and entrepreneurship, academics, the arts, health and fitness, language, music and technology. Instructors can use the site's course-development tools to upload video, PowerPoint presentations, PDFs and zip files to create courses. They can also engage and interact with users via online discussion boards.

Online learning sites are of course nothing new, with some of the first programs taking up web site residence as early as the late 1990s. But the sheer scope of sites like Udemy are a microcosm of the almost unlimited reach of the On Demand culture.

And speaking of scope…Bali has gone on to found a company called Carbon Health, dedicated to connecting patients with the right care in the online network. In a recent interview, Bali talked about the ability of On Demand companies like Carbon Health to empower consumers. He noted that, by integrating a healthcare practice with clinics, insurance companies, pharmacies, labs and medical imaging centers, patients become empowered, too. Specifically, Bali says, by using the service, individuals can schedule appointments, make payments, fill prescriptions and, crucially, access their medical records. "Instead of a health record system where patients' records are stored on the provider side, we flipped the system," he said.

Healthcare in the Age of Insights on Demand: Once slow to join the party, the industry is now a leading force

No industry has seen more change in recent years than healthcare. In the last two decades the global healthcare system has been transformed from a top-down, remote system to a dynamic, consumer-driven enterprise. An industry that was slow to understand and respond to the changing needs of the consumer now employs the most up-to-date tools and methodologies to harvest and interpret consumer insights. This changing geography in healthcare of course follows on the heels of similar changes in industries like travel, retail and banking…but in healthcare the consumer-driven revolution has been particularly dramatic.

The engine behind the revolution that has spread across healthcare (also encompassing related industries including bio-tech and pharmaceuticals) is of course the Internet. With the advent of sites like WedMD and Everyday Health, consumers suddenly had access to a universe of information about every medical condition imaginable. (Never was the old axiom "information is power" truer.) And with the rise of social media sites, a range of patient communities formed. In fact, today there are online communities for patients with every known condition. According to Dave Johnson, Managing Director Marketing Research, W2O Group, that rise in groups focused on rare diseases and newer diagnoses has been especially dramatic.

"There has been so much growth in educational resources for people with rare diseases, prompting the formation of very active communities," he says.

W2O's tagline says it all when it comes to its immersion in the world of Insights on Demand. "A marketing-communications firm driven by insight integration to give brands an unfair advantage." In the healthcare realm, the firm is helping clients "prioritize collaboration, data, and technology, enabling a true network of care… Highly regulated healthcare organizations can only break new ground by going deep to understand their audiences so they can reach them with actionable messages. W2O is doing just that for healthcare from the biggest companies to the world of startups."

Johnson says that, while it took some time for healthcare to rise to the occasion, marketers are now "going deep" to understand and target services to the newly empowered consumer. He notes that insight professionals are using a range of techniques, including, digital tracking, AI, machine learning and collaboration to meet health care consumers where they live—often in one of the patient forums that have sprung up all over the social media universe.

"Overall, the focus in healthcare today is indisputably on the consumer. Through interactions with patients and patient groups, insight professionals are able to provide a steady flow of new information. And, in turn, companies are able to target services to the specific needs of individual consumers," he notes.

Across the healthcare geography, insight gathering is becoming increasingly "granular," Johnson says, with widespread use of advanced segmentation techniques to help create a laser focus. This is true in every area of healthcare, including biotech and pharmaceuticals, where consumer insights are leading to important treatment advancements.

"We're seeing a continual increase in insights from multiple sources. More access to data means more insights, leading to more targeted products and services. And this process is going to continue, with constantly expanding sources of data and information leading to dramatic improvements in healthcare across the globe."

The Ever-Expanding On Demand Universe

We could almost literally go on forever recounting success stories in the On Demand universe. And, as technology continues to advance and a tech-savvy population around the globe demands more and more services online, the number of companies can only increase.

The power of consumers to drive the growth of the On Demand world actually has its roots in the development of one-to-one marketing. In the next chapter, we'll look at how that culture has worked to make the individual consumer the powerhouse behind the On Demand economy.

CHAPTER 6

At the Heart of It All: The Individual Consumer

At the heart of Insights on Demand is the drive across the global business geography to understand and appeal to consumers on an individual, one-to-one basis. As consumers develop deep profiles detailing their lives in the digital world, it becomes more and more routine to market to people based on their individual preferences and needs. And of course technological advancements (including Big Data, AI and blockchain—which we'll discuss in a later chapter) are making this approach available to even the smallest companies.

When you think about it, it only makes sense that real one-to-one marketing should develop in the online universe. In the digital domain marketers can interact with consumers in real-time, intervening with just the right information they need at given points in their digital journey. ***Obviously, this is beneficial to a brand, but it's also beneficial to a*** *consumer who may be having trouble translating needs and wants to action. (Once again the theme of democratization surfaces.)*

Marketers are now able to build what is being called dynamic creative (ads) custom-designed for specific people. Infectious Media defines this as "any creative that changes automatically based on information about the user, whether this is related to their behavior, location or context." First, a template for the ad or video is clearly defined within the dynamic system. Then, based on what the program knows about the recipient of the communications, the photo, product, offer, headline or any number of factors can be changed to provide that individual with the most relevant piece of communication. This can even be done with online video, where the algorithm edits together specific pieces of the video to serve up communication that checks off all the right elements for that particular viewer. This process creates digital communications that truly are one-to-one marketing messages.

And it's now possible to create predictive models that allow researchers to predict what a customer's most likely next purchase is, based on the products they have already bought. With this knowledge marketers can send them marketing messages that feature the product most likely to be next up in their purchase cycle. This gives them relevant messaging and helps move them through their buying journey that much quicker.

Essentially, marketers can now segment an audience to a market of one. This is the evolution of a form of marketing which, believe it or not, has actually been around since the very beginnings of commerce.

Back in the Beginning
One-to-one marketing (sometimes expressed as 1:1 marketing) has been around for a long time as a customer relationship management strategy emphasizing personalized interactions with customers. The concept of one-to-one marketing as a CRM approach was first advanced by Don Peppers and Martha Rogers in their 1994 book, *The One to One Future*.

But only the term is new; the approach is almost as old as commerce itself. In the past, for example, owners of a general store would naturally take a one-to-one approach, remembering details about each customer's preferences and characteristics and using that knowledge to provide better service. One-to-one marketing seeks to revitalize marketing with the personal touch absent from the marketing cycle for too long.

Peering into the Future

Back in 1993 Don Peppers and Martha Rogers were clearly peering into the future. Think about it: The Internet didn't yet exist, and yet the pair named and defined principles that are now dominating commerce on the web. They explained in the book why marketing should be about personalization and building real customer relationships. They knew even back then that real success lay in building a uniquely satisfying relationship with each customer—1 to 1!

In a recent interview, Peppers explained that before the advent of the net there was a range of attempts to use existing technology in 1:1 marketing. For example, there was a fax company that would send offers via fax, based on data they collected from a form you sent out and faxed to them. Of course the solution was far from efficient, but it shows that there was already a desire to send direct and personalized messages to customers.

Moving forward to today's market, Peppers calls personalization "the holy grail of marketing." But he notes that, while we have become accustomed to receiving personalized messages, they actually fit into a bigger picture that involves making any interaction with a brand as "frictionless" as possible. Now, he says, marketing should be all about creating the smoothest, most effortless and individual customer experience possible.

In fact, he says that customer experience is actually the greatest untapped source to decrease costs and increase revenue for most businesses. He points out that the most successful On Demand companies (Uber and Airbnb are good examples) have virtually NO tangible assets; the value they create is purely based on their customers. **In the final analysis, Peppers says success in the On Demand world is not about how many customers you reach, but how many customer needs you have satisfied.**

The constantly increasing emphasis on the individual might make you think communities as a critical market research tool are a thing of the past. Not true! In fact, communities are an integral part of the contemporary social experience. Across the online universe, consumers find support and a sense of belonging in communities of every kind. That makes them valuable to consumers of every stripe and increasingly important tools for insight professionals and brand marketers.

Communities: Alive and Well in Today's New World Order

Good news: Consumer communities are alive and well and an integral part of market research in the new age of on-demand business. In fact, communities are perfectly suited to support the new paradigm for on-the-spot decision making that now characterizes the business landscape. Obviously, that's good news to insights professionals, who traditionally have looked to consumers for real-world views of products and concepts. But it's REALLY good news for manufacturers and brand marketers who now, more than ever, need to put the consumer in the heart of every decision they make.

In these days of hypercompetition and accelerated decision making, consumer research is no longer a zero-sum game, with researchers conducting massive studies and seeking yes or no answers at the end of development processes. Instead, insight professionals and stakeholders across an organization need support from the very beginning of a project and throughout development, to support on-the-spot decision making. In the new business paradigm, researchers seek to test and learn all along the development continuum, and today's communities are perfectly suited to that need.

Here's why:

Communities are an integral part of the contemporary social experience. Across the online universe, consumers find support and a sense of belonging in communities of every kind. That makes it very natural for them to participate in branded communities; they are happy to engage in communities that extend their online experiences and offer more information about the products they use in their daily lives. And thanks to ubiquitous mobile technology, consumers are available for engagements at a moment's notice. That makes it easy for researchers to quickly mount a short-term community to support on-the-spot decision making. So, in addition to traditional communities, which are long-term engagements, marketers now can bring together small, targeted communities to answer questions about concept or packaging design, giving them the security they need to move forward in the development process.

And easy access to online communities has made companies of every kind add them to their research arsenal. Even brands that are often invisible to consumers, or low-engagement products, are turning to communities for support in decision making. In fact, companies that may have chosen other research methods in the past are now finding that access to online consumer communities provides just the support they need throughout today's accelerated product-development process.

As confirmation of the value of today's consumer communities, in the 2017 GRIT report, 82 percent of consumer insights professionals stated that they're currently using or considering communities. Clearly, communities have continued to thrive because their value is unquestioned in the new business environment, where researchers need both quantitative data and qualitative insights throughout the development projects. Communities offer views of their products that are simply unavailable anywhere else. What's more, they haven't stopped evolving; they continue to incorporate new techniques, such as digital tracking, social listing and diary studies, and can be quicker than ever to launch.

Today, brand marketers and stakeholders across the organization want the security only varied input throughout the development process can bring. And in the online, On Demand, uberfied environment they need questions answered instantly. Modern, online communities give insight professionals and brand marketers just the agility they need to provide ongoing, varied input throughout a product or concept development process.

In essence, today's online/mobile consumer communities are proving to be the agile, nimble partners companies need to compete effectively. They are indeed alive and well and thriving in the On Demand marketplace.

Individual consumers—whether they're involved in their own online journeys or as part of communities—are at the heart of the effort to bring together all the tools insight professionals and businesspeople need to equip them for the On Demand universe. The resulting mega-tool—and the ultimate democratization of the marketplace—lay in Insights on Demand, which stands as the amalgamation of all the tools and methodologies best suited to the marketplace of the future. In the final chapter, we'll do a little futurecasting, painting a picture of the New Age of Market Research.

CHAPTER 7

Futurecasting: Meeting Unimaginable Complexity with Insights on Demand

In essence, this book is all about change. And, as the old axiom goes, one thing we can count on is change. We all know that a number of factors—including advanced technology, global competition and price constraints—have changed the marketplace forever. But the degree of change in markets around the world has been staggering and makes a discussion of change almost impossibly complex. In fact, these days, as soon as you finish a report on almost any subject—including change—the report is obsolete.

Nowhere are the effects of change being felt more strongly than in market research. In the past, we have worked to understand the needs of consumers and translate those needs and desires to our clients. It was, in fact, a fairly direct relationship; we have met consumers where they lived—in shopping malls or in their homes via phone and inevitably online—used our expertise to ask the right questions, then provided analysis for our clients. It was a process everyone understood, and for years it provided businesses with the market intelligence they needed to give their most important customers what they wanted and answer key questions about their brand.

With the advent of the Internet, everything began to change; individual consumers began to explore a whole new online universe, expanding their worlds in the process. But the real explosion came with the spread of social media. Essentially, consumers have found new online homes in sites like Facebook and Instagram and support groups across the web.

And the real clincher is of course mobile technology. (Think about it: Do you even know anyone without a cell phone today?) Take a look at the people around you on a train or subway car: a vast majority are on their phones. What that means is that they are not JUST on the train; they are also on Facebook connecting with friends, in an aisle at Walmart and in their office responding to a client's message. Virtually no one exists only in the single dimension of the physical world anymore. We are now multi-dimensional beings with virtual homes all over the online universe, creating what might be best called a blended reality.

For brand marketers and market research professionals, that has made the task of understanding the consumer's journey almost unimaginably complex. For one thing, the sheer size of a consumer's world has expanded to include countless online destinations, as well as geographical locales like retail outlets. So insight professionals need to be equipped to gather and analyze the constantly swelling tide of data. And here's the key point: While it used to take some time for a complex journey to develop, it now happens instantaneously, as a consumer moves seamlessly from the real world to the digital universe and back again. Researchers must now be able to understand a consumer's whole ecosystem and travel seamlessly across its borders in real time. That of course means employing advanced technology that allows a researcher to go along for the ride from a mobile device, to another device without limitation; in other words, a researcher or brand marketer needs to be able to instantly be immersed in the consumer's journey.

It's Only Going to Get Worse

As we said at the beginning of this chapter, the rate of change in the marketplace—and everywhere else—will only continue to accelerate. For one thing, as consumers in the developing world begin to charge up their digital devices, there will be an exponential increase in the amount and kind of data populating various clouds.

Added to the increased number of consumers entering the digital marketplace is the fact that technology will only continue to advance. Way back in the middle of the last century, Gordon E. Moore predicted that technology—symbolized by the complexity of integrated circuits—would continually advance and increase. While various pundits have predicted that the march of tech would eventually slow down, there are no real signs that will happen any time soon. And new forms of technology are certain to significantly expand users' access to new realities in the online universe.

The hyper-explosion of consumer data out there demands that insight professionals and businesses stay well ahead of the curve. It seems clear that the future of market research will be all about the virtually complete elimination of limits. For example, while reaching out to consumers one-at-a-time to gauge individual tastes and needs, we will have the capacity to reach out through online and mobile surveys to an almost unlimited population of consumers. We have to be capable of gathering multiple layers of data in real time, then seamlessly integrating powerful analytics, instantly delivering actionable insights. That of course means adopting more and more technology, with automated systems already enabling once-unimaginable capabilities.

Even more amazingly, we are no longer limited to simply reported data; new technologies now make it possible to understand how REAL thoughts and beliefs impact behavior. Through a number of methodologies that make up the discipline behavioral economics, researchers are pushing at the boundaries of the possible by measuring actual behavior and thoughts, rather than assessing stated behaviors and thoughts.

Tapping the Unconscious—A Whole New Universe of Data

Market research has traditionally rested on the foundation of reported data which—as recent research is proving—can be subject to cognitive biases. So despite best efforts to accurately report behavior, actual behavior and decision making can be very different from what people think or say they will do under given circumstances. So, more and more researchers are using a range of methods to actually monitor unconscious reaction to market stimuli, in a new area of research now commonly termed behavioral economics.

It should come as no surprise to any of us that we don't always make rational decisions, with many of our decisions driven by rapid, nonconscious, intuitive thought, sometimes called System 1 thinking. A whole range of new technologies is now being tested and used to measure these thought patterns, including facial coding, biometric response, eye tracking and Implicit Reaction Time (IRT), which measures the length of time it takes for a respondent to answer a specific question; the faster the response, the stronger the presumed conviction. Neuroscience and facial coding techniques seem to be good fits for messages that have extended time exposure, such as TV ads or political speeches, when you want to measure change in emotion over time. On the other hand, IRT can be integrated into a traditional survey without special equipment.

A number of experts are working on developing and assessing these techniques on a number of fronts. One example is neuro-marketing expert Martin Lindstrom, whose book, *Buyology* recounts his three-year study to determine what kinds of advertising actually elicited measureable response in subjects' brains. He used clinical tests including MRIs to provide actual measurements of brain response to a variety of stimuli, with some surprising results.

For example, cigarette warnings actually activate the parts of the brain that derive pleasure from smoking. And a 2007 brain-scan study showed that viewers were actually half as likely to remember a sex-based advertisement compared to a normal ad. (Apparently the brain was distracted by the idea of sex itself and missed remembering the product of brand involved.) On the other hand, product integration, memorable phrases or iconic product mascots, and odor-based advertising proved to be very effective, creating easily accessed pathways in the brain that make for memorable and effective brands.

Tests like these are proving that neuroscience techniques can help researchers assess how a stimulus, such as an ad or consumer message, elicits emotions, and can even tell us what kinds of emotions. This is critical because we know that emotions are the primary driver of many decisions we make, so the better we can test actual emotional response, the better we can understand the impact on consumer decisions. However, again, these approaches can be limiting. Unlike in a survey, they don't allow you the chance to go deeper into what a consumer is thinking and feeling—to get the "why" behind a consumer's emotions and behavior.

Despite limitations, forays into the world of neuroscience are only going to continue, as researchers continue their search for ways of peering into the human psyche. And, although it may seem counterintuitive, studies of observed behavior are often considered less intrusive than studies of reported data, because subjects aren't asked to put their lives on hold to record reactions.

And it only makes sense that researchers should integrate behavioral profiling and big data sources with survey methods to get a more holistic picture of the consumer and the effectiveness of marketing campaigns. This of course involves digital tracking, along with the use of GPS tracking and frequent shopper accounts. In these cases, participants also agree to take surveys, which when layered with the behavioral data, allow researchers to run tests that assess the impact of marketing stimulus on both sales and consumer perceptions and better understand each consumer's journey.

This attention to the needs and wants of the individual consumer is another sure sign of the growing democratization of market research. And yet another sign is the drive among consumers to gain control of their own data, even in the age of Big Data, as amounts of information continue to grow to almost unimaginable proportions.

A Chain of Data Warehouses
One way consumers are looking to retain the key to their own data is through the advent of blockchain technology. Originally developed as the distributed transaction ledgers on which cryptocurrencies like Bitcoin are tracked, these ledgers are allowing consumers to lock away their personal data in data warehouses and encode the key. This affords consumers complete control of their data, while providing researchers with a means to directly access a 360-degree view of a consumer motivated to share her data.

According to Frank Smadja, Executive Vice President of Technology at Toluna, "Permissioned blockchains will boil down to faster, more efficient transfer and storage of information. In the end, both researchers and marketers will have access to accurate, quantifiable information that can be used to gather insights."

In fact, blockchain is becoming the gold standard for trusted, secure transactions because the information is completely secure and unchangeable. That can positively impact an insight professional's life in a number of ways. For example, it will no longer be necessary to take a respondent's word that he qualifies for a survey; the proof is in his blockchain data. And even more enticingly, each time a consumer makes a transaction—whether related to a survey or not—their new information will become part of their permanent record. So a researcher will know that a respondent participated in a drug-related survey three years before AND that they purchased a related medicine just last week. And researchers will be able to initiate automatic cryptocurrency payments to ensure that participants are compensated for participation in a survey.

Bottom line: In this age of hyper-development, previous limits no longer apply. For example, old limitations like the Iron Triangle pick-two rule are being virtually obliterated.

Faster, Better, Cheaper—Now a Reality in Consumer Insights
There is a concept in the project management realm that has dominated thinking since at least the 1950s. The Iron Triangle states that any attempt to achieve a positive outcome is constrained by the three variables of

time, cost and *scope*. Or, in popular vernacular, in attempting to produce anything new, a team is always looking to create something *faster, better* and *cheaper*. Since the concept saw the light of day more than sixty years ago, one of its iron-clad tenets has been that in any endeavor a team has to "pick two." The thinking has always been that it's impossible to produce something that is—all at once—faster, better and cheaper.

Well, like so many other notions that developed back in the last century, the Iron Triangle is fading into memory. And, as in so many other cases where old ideas are being blown out of the water, it's the power of advanced technology that's melting the Iron Triangle away. One industry where this is playing out with dramatic results is consumer insights, and the results are proving to be literally transformative; thanks to a cadre of advanced technologies, resting on a foundation of expertise, insights are now being delivered to clients in record time (faster), with more actionable data (better), and at reduced unit cost (cheaper).

Everything has changed.

Meeting Consumers Where They Live (Faster)

Thanks to the spread and advancement of mobile technology—and the use of advanced technologies like digital tracking—consumer insights professionals are able to meet consumers where they live in the digital world. They are able to join a consumer on a digital journey, instantly recording the experience and impressions. And automated, platform approaches to market research—which automate the whole range of critical market research functions—offer the speed and agility needed to keep pace with constantly changing consumer sentiments.

This is especially critical as whole population groups of consumers in Africa and Asia join the digital universe. In the consumer insights industry, that means hundreds of millions more consumer touch points and the almost unimaginable complexity of matching the right surveys with the consumers. Despite this ever-growing level of complexity, clients need answers faster than ever before to remain competitive. The industry is keeping pace with that exploding demand by employing systems that not only mine reservoirs of data, but also instantly apply advanced analytics.

✓ Faster

Machine Learning Layered on Big Data (Better)

Consumer insights professionals now have access to almost unlimited stores of consumer data, offering detailed, granular views of individual consumers. And, most importantly, by layering in machine learning (AI) they can instantly see patterns of behavior, leading to all-important predictions of future behavior. That means they can instantly zero in on the data that's going to be most predictive and actionable.

✓ Better

Automation Means Lower Costs

Automation—and especially integrated platform solutions—have made it not only possible, but cost-effective to keep pace with the demand for instant consumer insights. Now, rather than bringing on new personnel, consumer insights professionals and marketers are turning to automated platform solutions like TolunaInsights to cost-effectively garner actionable data from hundreds of millions of data points, while also applying advanced analytics.

✓ Cheaper

Advanced technologies now driving the consumer insights space have made the "pick two" rule a thing of the past.

What It All Means for Insight Professionals—AND Businesspeople

The challenge will of course be to store and manage SO MUCH data. Clearly that means that cloud technology and AI (and whatever else is new on the horizon) will continue to be invaluable research tools and necessary aids in promoting the democratization of market research.

Take a look at the video I recorded a few years ago to demonstrate how the whole range of market research tools and techniques are coming together to promote the democratization of the industry.
https://www.youtube.com/watch?reload=9&v=-4Jnvz_9coI

As the market continues to change, insight professionals will of course be employing an ever-increasing number of technologies to enable dynamically-generated insights, including artificial intelligence to provide powerful analytics. And there is another dimension to the advancements in the delivery of insights: market research expertise is being seamlessly integrated into the process, so businesspeople now have access to a hybrid system that combines insight delivery with market research—all available On Demand whenever a business person needs it.

While almost everything has changed, in the age of Insights on Demand, one thing remains constant: We're there to give businesses the intelligence they need to deal with anything the changing markets can throw at them.

APPENDIX

About the Insights on Demand Consortium

In November 2017, ITWP, parent company of Toluna and Harris Interactive, launched the Insights on Demand Consortium, an industry-wide member consortium. Since its inception, the consortium has grown constantly and now includes consumer insights and marketing professionals representing some of the world's most recognized consumer brands. Together they have laid the groundwork for the organization, participated in industry events, and addressed core topics facing the industry, including agility and speed, big data and data science, the role of customer experience in market research, and automation. They stand at the vanguard of the industry's constantly accelerating drive into the age of Insights on Demand.

Since its founding, the Consortium has attracted participants from Fortune 500 and other leading brands across all industries and geographies, who share their excitement about collaborating openly and sharing their opinions, experiences, and challenges with fellow members. While the group is comprised of a diverse group of professionals, members share the common goal of further evolving, refining, and promoting innovative ways to gain and distribute market insights.

At a recent Consortium meeting, members focused on the implementation of agile research programs, digging deep into the support of quick-turn, fast-fail decision making, in addition to exploring the marriage of behavioral data and consumer insights.

In fact, I'm constantly encouraged by the growth, ongoing collaboration and dialogue we've had between members. Together we are forging inroads around the continued evolution of the insights industry and our vision to democratize market research. In the process, we are continually providing our business clients with the most up-to-date approaches to insight gathering and analysis available. After all, the ultimate vision for Insights on Demand is to democratize market research, making consumer insights and behavior accessible to all business professionals in companies of all sizes.

Here is a link to see a list of the members of the Consortium, which now numbers more than 100. https://www.insightsondemand.org/members

The Consortium Takes Root
Here is a snapshot of responses to the Consortium across various industries. Below are excerpts from discussions at the group's UK launch:

Discussions at the launch centered around three topics:

- Agility and Speed and Automation

- Big Data and Data Science

- MR vs CX

Agility and Speed and Automation
How do we as an industry become more agile, iterative and nimble, without forsaking a commitment to quality?

The **demand for speed can't be ignored,** and where possible quicker approaches are needed and required from the business otherwise clients will seek information elsewhere or not at all. This is extremely challenging for purists and research experts. In the end, limited information in real time is better than more comprehensive information after the decision needs to be taken. The essential point to remember, attendees determined, is that **the purpose of MR is to inform. This important role can't be replaced by automation but it can help speed up some of the processes in the project lifecycle. In the end, there shouldn't be agile or not agile research – it all should be agile and high quality. These days, insight professionals have to consistently counter the viewpoint that speed equals poor quality.**

Key points from the discussions:

- Consumer motivations may change less often than we think they do; however, there may be a time where brands are focusing or offering services that digitally native customers don't necessarily value. A focused Fintech business, for example, could just deliver a particular niche customers want.

- Historic segmentations which may no longer maximize value can be embedded in an organization. Updating and evolving segmentation and proving its value needs to be an iterative and agile process and can incorporate many factors: demographic, behavioral, attitudinal, emotional, etc.

- There are also instances when segmentation/segments don't match the behavioral data too well, which adds to the challenge of getting the right message to the right people. Indications that brands are working on more attitudinal profiling to add that dimension and enhance all this ….and recognition that the 'perfect' data only/ statistics driven segmentation doesn't often work best anyway – has to 'land' with stakeholders/make sense and be actionable and targetable, so it can be accepted and embedded within the business and 'live' for some time.

- Brands are getting more savvy in terms of using and blending segmentations for targeting – comparing or blending their own segmentations with similar insights that agencies can offer.

- **Automation** provides something that wasn't possible before and frees up the MR team to add value. How do MR/insight teams navigate between automated products or custom products – when should they be used/not used? For example, if an automated concept test takes just two days, how is it credible and how can internal stakeholders be persuaded? Attendees suggested that the team could conduct a test between an automated product and a traditional one as a proof test.

Big Data and Data Science

Will big data and data science make market research obsolete, or can they empower a vibrant new era for the industry? Attendees determined that, in fact, the opportunity with big data is huge. There was general agreement that it is exciting for researchers to have access to so much information. However, experts need to make sense of the data, to establish the issues and questions that need answering. Big data can often tell you what is happening but not why.

Key points from the discussions:

- A small but representative sample could be better than 250,000 tweets, despite the fact that some view bigger data sets as inherently better.

- It's easy to track clicks/purchase/other metrics, but this tells you little or nothing about the impact on feelings towards the brand. It's important to recognize the limitations of data.

- The answer may be to have data that has both breadth and depth, for example, using a mix of transactional, cookie, survey and social data to build brand value.

CX vs MR

How can MR adapt as gathering data on the customer journey becomes part of many other roles and functions, not just the research team?

CX is an opportunity that MR needs to embrace. It can be difficult to navigate as the internal processes and systems often make mapping the customer journey and experience extremely difficult. However, the data does need to be integrated and customer expectations need to be included as part of the process.

Key points from the discussions:

- CX has evolved into a specialist discipline that sits outside of research (team/activity?) and has left MR behind, to some degree. This is leading to creative tensions with MR and silos of data, insight and expertise. Therefore, putting this together for the overall story/narrative is difficult.

- Customer knowledge for digital companies could be incredibly granular, for example game playing online, games played, hours played.

- Granular behavioral data doesn't answer the why. You just see what people did. Therefore, we need to develop segments that combine the CRM data with motivational data.

- Perhaps CX methodologies have developed and spread because traditional MR tools have not always served clients well.

- It's important to build trust with the consumer at all points in the customer journey.

Consortium members have continued to meet in forums like the one described above and are proving to be important allies in the industry's drive to fully adopt Insights on Demand.